APSA
Style Manual
for
Political Science

Revised August 2006

American Political Science Association
Committee on Publications

This most recent, 2006 revision of the *Style Manual for Political Science* is predicated upon the publication of the 15th edition of the *Chicago Manual of Style*. The *Style Manual* still takes as its base the changes in the style of the *American Political Science Review* during the editorship of Ada Finifter (1996–2001).

Revisions to this edition were made by Polly Karpowicz and Steve Yoder. Thanks to *American Political Science Review* Editor Lee Sigelman for his contribution to this edition. Revisions to the 2001 edition were made by Theresa Gubicza Souther, Ed Lamb, and Blake Brunner and reviewed by several editors political science journal editors and final manuscript edits were supervised by Lee Sigelman, who began editorship of the *American Political Science Review* in 2002.

Additional copies of the manual can be obtained through the American Political Science Association, online at www.apsanet.org.

Copyright 2006 by the American Political Science Association. All rights reserved. ISBN 1-87814-733-1

TABLE OF CONTENTS

FOREWORD 5

INTRODUCTION 8

SUBMISSION POLICY 9

SUBMISSION FORM 11
    Length 11
    Order of Contents 11
    Headings 12

TEXT STYLE 12
    Acronyms and Abbreviations 12
    Compound Words 12
    Equations and Variables 13
    Gender-Neutral Language 13
    I or We? 14
    Numbers 14
    Possessives 15
    Roman, Italics, or Quotation Marks? 15
    Spacing 16
    That or Which? 16
    Titles and Terms 16

CITATIONS 17
    Chronology 18
    Multiple Authors and Works 18
    Older Works 19
    Government Documents 20
    Data Archived and Available at the Inter-university Consortium for Political and Social Research (ICPSR) 20
    Electronic Sources 21

APPENDIXES 21

NOTES 22
    Interviews and Personal Communications 23
    Newspaper Articles 23

REFERENCES 24
    Books 24

Journal Articles 26
Unpublished Works 27
Older Works... 27
Government Documents 28
Data Archived And Available at the Inter-university Consortium for Political and Social Research (ICPSR).................................... 30
Electronic Sources 31
English Translations.. 32
Sources in Other Languages.. 32
Magazine Articles.. 33

TABLES AND FIGURES.. 33
Tables.. 33
Figures.. 36

APPENDIX TO STYLE MANUAL... 37
Data Sources and Archived Data for Articles Accepted for Publication in the *American Political Science Review* 37

Submission Guidelines to APSA Journals
American Political Science Review................................... 38
Perspectives on Politics 41
PS: Political Science & Politics 46

Foreword
Note to Authors of Articles Accepted for Publication in the *American Political Science Review*
by Lee Sigelman,
Editor of *American Political Science Review*

Like merchants, mechanics, and medical doctors, political scientists use specialized vocabularies and sophisticated methods to draw distinctions among, and to try to enhance their understanding of, the complex phenomena in which we are interested. These are double-edged swords. Just as they can help advance knowledge, they can foreclose communication among all but a small band of cognoscenti.

The *American Political Science Review* (*APSR*) is a professional journal, not a mass-circulation magazine meant to be readily comprehensible to those untutored in political science. To be sure, key findings or insights from some *APSR* articles diffuse rapidly, informing classroom discussion and op-ed columns and contributing to public understanding and policy debates. In many other instances, though, such diffusion occurs only gradually, if at all.

Scholars who submit manuscripts to *APSR* are asserting, in effect, that they have something unusually interesting and important to tell their colleagues—and eventually, perhaps, to tell the world. *APSR* is hardly the only available publication outlet, but as the research journal of the American Political Science Association it is an especially prominent one. Only a small fraction (one-tenth or less in recent decades) of the manuscripts that are submitted to it survive its rigorous peer-review process. To do so, they must be analytically sound; poorly constructed arguments, weak research designs, and porous evidence are not the stuff of which *APSR* articles are made. An article is published in *APSR* only when those involved in the peer-review process consider it representative of the best work being done in political science and only when they deem it sufficiently important to be brought to the attention of *APSR*'s broad, pan- and inter-disciplinary readership.

A style manual is not the place to launch a consideration of what constitutes the "best work," other than to say that political science is an extremely diverse discipline and that *APSR* is eager to publish work representing a wide array of theoretical orientations, methodological approaches, and substantive interests. Rather, the purpose of this manual is to provide guidelines for the effective communication of research in political science. Many of the matters discussed here are minor, bordering on trivial. (Does a "p." precede the page number in an in-text citation?) Some should not have to be discussed at all, but experience suggests that they must be. (What is the difference between "that" and "which"?) Many, however, when understood in a broader context, are central to the scholarly enterprise. (How does one appropriately acknowledge the contributions of others?)

Unfortunately, there can be no guarantee of effective communication even when an author scrupulously follows all the stylistic guidelines that are spelled out below. Each author is likely to be more conversant than all but a few readers with the theoretical context, prior research, data, and methods that come into play in a particular project. Too many authors expect too much of their potential readers at the outset, thereby unduly narrowing the audience for their work. (The opposite mistake occurs when authors expect too little, moving so far back toward first principles that their manuscripts read more like primers for the uninitiated than straightforward presentations of sophisticated pieces of research.) In drafting articles, I often find it useful to identify in the very first sentence the central issue I am going to consider, generally by stating it in the form of a question. Then, in the next few sentences, I try to explain in the clearest language possible why this question is of great interest and importance. Many journalists believe that if they get the "lead" right, an article will almost write itself, and also that a good lead will hook prospective readers. Political scientists seem to find this difficult, in part because we tend to ask more complicated questions and in part because, unlike journalists, getting the lead right is not something we have been trained to do. The unfortunate consequence is that too often our work does not attract the readership that it deserves.

It is the obligation of authors to make their research accessible to prospective readers, not by "dumbing it down" but by effectively conveying what they are trying to find out and why this quest is so worthwhile. Following the guidelines spelled out in this manual will be a step in that direction, but the real key lies in careful editing and rewriting designed to open lines of communication rather than to close them.

It is not reasonable to expect researchers who use complex formal or statistical models to conduct tutorials on their methods as a part of reporting their work; or to hold those whose research focuses on a certain nation or a certain political thinker responsible for introducing the rest of us to the most basic aspects of their subject matter before turning to the specific issues of concern; or, more generally, to require researchers to eschew all but plain, simple English. Moreover, it is naive to expect that, having been hooked by a good lead, those who are untrained in formal or statistical modeling will suddenly become avid and knowledgeable consumers of the technical portions of a statistical or formal presentation, or that those who had previously shown little or no interest in a certain region or thinker will suddenly yearn to master the subtlest nuances thereof. But it is neither unreasonable nor naive to insist at the very least that as political scientists we can and should clearly communicate to a broad range of other political scientists what we are trying to do and why it matters.

Let me close with a few words to student users of this manual. The basic skills that you need in order to write a successful research paper follow directly from commonsensical rules like "Organize your ideas logically," "Build transitions from one point to the next," "Make your points concisely," and "Edit, edit, edit." If you don't know these rules, learn them, for they will stand you in good stead for the rest of your life. If you know them but don't practice them, change your ways.

Unfortunately, if your research is unsound in the first place, following these rules — let alone mastering the specifics of *APSR* format — won't help you much, and it could even make matters worse: when you present your work clearly, you run the risk of bringing its deficiencies out into the open for all to see. What is certain, though, is that even the very best research will fall flat if it is poorly presented. You should resist any temptation to treat the write-up casually, as an incidental add-on after the "real" work of doing research is over. It is an integral, crucial component of the research process, but one that unfortunately receives too little attention from neophytes and practicing professionals alike.

Introduction

The more care an author exerts in preparing a work, the less it will be subject to well-meaning "improvements" by copy editors. Attention paid to both literary and editorial style—clear expression and consistent usage—will produce professional published work that has remained under the author's control.

In matters of editorial style, APSA follows the latest edition of the **Chicago Manual of Style (CMS)**. Numbers referring to the appropriate chapters and sections of the manual's fifteenth edition appear in the guidelines here. Use the Merriam-Webster dictionaries, specifically the latest edition of Webster's New Collegiate Dictionary and the older unabridged edition of Webster's Third New International Dictionary, as the standard for spelling, capitalization, and hyphenation. In addition, the English-German volume (volume 1) of Wolfgang J. Koschnick's Standard Dictionary of the Social Sciences provides an exhaustive and invaluable reference for spelling, capitalization, and hyphenation of social science terms.

Submission Policy

Authors should not submit manuscripts that contain substantial amounts of text or data that have already been published, are forthcoming, or are included in other manuscripts submitted for review,. This rule applies to books or periodicals (including online journals). Copies of manuscripts are not returned.

The American Political Science Review strongly discourages submission of articles that are substantially similar to manuscripts submitted or published elsewhere, or to part of a book or other larger work. It is the author's responsibility to discuss any such related publications in a cover letter to the editor. The author should also notify the editor of any pertinent submissions to other publishers, whether for book or periodical publication, that occur while an article is under review. Copies of related publications may be requested.

General Submission Procedures
(See the appendix for submission guidelines for APSA journals)

1. Submit five copies of manuscripts. Review each copy to make sure it contains all tables, figures, appendices, and references mentioned in the manuscript and that all pages are legible.

2. To comply with the policy of double-blind peer review, only one copy should be fully identified as to authorship. For anonymous copies, if an author's previous publications are cited, this should be done in a way that does not make the authorship of the submitted paper obvious. This is most easily accomplished by referring to oneself in the third person and including normal references to the work cited in the list of references. Assuming that text references to an author's previous work are in third person, full citations should be included as usual in the bibliography. Use of other procedures to render manuscripts anonymous should be discussed with the editor prior to submission. Authors should not thank colleagues in notes or elsewhere in the body of the paper or mention institution names, web page addresses, or other identifying

information. All acknowledgments must appear only on the title page of the identified copy. Manuscripts that are not judged anonymous will not be reviewed.

3. Cover pages: The first page of the anonymous copies should contain only the title and the abstract. The first page of the identified copy should contain the name, institutional affiliation, and contact information for all authors (and in the case of multiple authors, an indication of the author who will receive correspondence); any relevant citations to the author's previous work that have been omitted from the anonymous copies; and acknowledgments, including the names of any colleagues who have provided comments on the manuscript. If the identified copy contains any unique references or is worded differently in any way, please mark this copy with "Contains author citations" at the top of the first page. Include a loose copy of the cover page of the identified copy as well.

Manuscripts that are largely or entirely critiques of, or commentaries on, previously published articles will be reviewed using the same general procedures as for regular articles, with one exception. In addition to the usual number of reviewers, such manuscripts will also be sent to the scholar(s) whose work is being reviewed, in the same anonymous form as they are sent to other reviewers. Comments from the original author(s) to the editor will be invited as a supplement to the advice of regular reviewers. This notice to the original author(s) encourages the review of the details of analyses or research procedures that might escape the notice of other reviewers. Authors of critiques should therefore send as many additional copies of their manuscripts as will be required for this purpose.

As part of the review process, authors may be asked to submit additional documentation if procedures (for example, techniques employed in data collection or analysis) are not sufficiently clear; the review process works most efficiently if such information is given in the initial submission. If readers are advised that additional information is available from the author, printed copies of that information should be submitted with the manuscript.

Submission Form

Title and Abstract

The title should be descriptive and short (12 words maximum, preferably fewer). On a separate sheet of paper, include an abstract of no more than 150 words succinctly describing the research problem investigated, the method for solving the problem, and the findings or conclusions presented. The abstract should summarize, not introduce, the manuscript.

Length

Use at least 11 point font for all parts of the paper. Manuscripts should be printed on one side of the paper only. Margins must be 1 ½ inches on all sides, and the right margin should not be justified. Many journals, including APSR, will not consider for review a manuscript that exceeds 45 double-spaced 8 ½ by 11 inch pages, including the title page, abstract, text, appendices, notes, references, tables, and figures.

Order of Contents

All parts of a manuscript should be double-spaced and should appear in the following order, each beginning on a new page, sequentially numbered from the title page:

1. Title page, with abstract (identifying information on one copy only)
2. Text
3. Appendix, if necessary
4. Notes, if necessary (for submission and review purposes, authors are encouraged to use footnotes; manuscripts accepted for publication must be submitted with endnotes)
5. References
6. Tables, titled and numbered, each on a separate page (for submission and review purposes, locate tables [only one to a page] approximately where they fall in the text);
7. Figures, titled and numbered, each on a separate page (for submission and review purposes, locate figures approximately

where they fall in the text).

Headings

Use three orders of headings in the manuscript, in both upper- and lowercase letters: Center primary headings, in boldface; place secondary headings flush left, in boldface; tertiary heads should be underlined and flush left, with headline style capitalization and a period at the end:

Primary Heading
Secondary Heading
<u>Tertiary Heading.</u> Text follows immediately.

When an article is typeset for publication, a different format may be used by the journal that accepted it.

Text Style

Acronyms and Abbreviations

Acronyms should be in parentheses at the first reference, following the spelled-out full form. In later references, the letters suffice. Two-letter acronyms for the 50 states may be used throughout the text. Names of countries should be spelled out in the text and abbreviated in tight matter. The abbreviation U.S. is acceptable in names of government institutions; but as a noun, United States is preferable. Avoid computer acronyms when referring to variables used in, or explaining results of, statistical analysis.

Very common abbreviations like dept. may be used in parentheses and tight matter. Scholarly abbreviations like e.g. and i.e.–in roman, not italic, type—may be used throughout the text.

Compound Words

A compound word consists of two (or more) words in any combination of nouns and adjectives (and some adverbs that look like adjectives) that together form either a noun or an adjective. Hyphenation draws the elements of a compound word closer together. A compound functioning as a noun and not found in the dictionary should not be hyphenated unless it falls into the category of one of the exceptions found in the *Chicago Manual of Style* (*CMS*) (7.90). More information can be found in *CMS* (7.82–7.90).

Equations and Variables

Number only displayed equations that are referred to directly in the text, notes, or appendix. The fewer numbered equations, the easier for the reader to follow explicit cross-referencing. Moreover, if all equations are numbered, the copy editors of most journals will delete some numbers and renumber the rest, with a substantial danger of confusion along the way.

All variables that appear in any tables or figures should be mentioned in the text. The first mention of each variable in the text is italicized (e.g., *age, gender, education*). In a discussion of general concepts, do not italicize the concepts. Italicization should be applied only to measured variables, and only the first time they are mentioned; thereafter, variable names are treated as normal text. Use terminology consistently: do not refer to the same variable by different names when discussing findings. The names of variables used in tables should match those in the text.

Gender-Neutral Language

Avoid inappropriately gender-specific language, including gender-specific terms for groups of people or the characterization of groups as male or female.

The following are some ways to avoid the most common sexist language trap, the use of *he, him,* or *his* as the default pronoun:

1. Replace *his* with *the, a,* or *personal,* or simply delete it.
2. Replace the pronoun with a common noun (e.g., *this individual, this citizen*).
3. Recast conditional sentences into sentences with *who* or

which: "If an individual votes, he participates," becomes "An individual who votes participates."
4. Convert the sentence to the plural

Three other techniques are possible but only at some sacrifice of style:

5. Replace *he* with *he* or *she*, and so on. (Do not alternate *he* and *she*, and do not simply use *she* instead of *he*.)
6. Convert the sentence to the passive voice.

The secret of editing to avoid sexist language is *variety*—usually a mix of the first three or four tactics. Consider the following sentence:

> The *congressman's* staff is itself intimately involved in his committee participation, keeping *him* briefed on committee activities. It looks out for *his* interests and often acts on *his* behalf. Information it provides *him* is often an important basis for *his* perception of a bill.

Edited it becomes:

> The staff is intimately involved in the committee work of its *representative, whom it keeps* briefed on committee activities. It looks out for *the member's* interests and often acts on *his or her* behalf. Information it provides is thus often an important basis for *the representative's* perception of a bill.

I or We?

Individual authors should refer to themselves as *I*. Use *we* only for joint authors. Self-effacement by means of the third person *(this author)* usually sounds unnatural or affected and author's references to themselves by surname (except for purposes of anonymity) even more so.

Numbers

Spelling Out Numbers. In the text, spell out *one* through *nine*. Use Arabic figures for other numbers (*CMS* 9.6). Percentages are expressed as figures followed by % even if the numeral is less than 10 (*CMS*

9.19). Always write out a number if it begins a sentence; if this seems awkward, recast the sentence.

Inclusive Numbers. Use of an *en dash* (as used in the examples below) between inclusive numbers signifies *up to and including*. Use an *en dash* between inclusive numbers (*CMS* 6.83).

To write inclusive numbers, omit the initial unchanged digits of the second numbers as long as they are not part of an unbreakable pair *(3–10; 105–6; 321–25; 415–532; 11,564–68)* (*CMS* 9.64).

Inclusive years can normally be treated in the same way (the words *years* being understood) unless *from* or *between* precedes the dates (*CMS* 5.115, 8.68):

> *the years 1944–47, war of 1914–18, during 1878–85, the 1878–1910 period*

but

> *from 1914 to 1918, between 1879 and 1902.*

Possessives

All one-syllable singular names and common nouns form possessives with *'s* (*sauce's, fox's, Zeus's*). All singular names and common nouns ending in an *s* or *z* sound and consisting of three or more syllables form possessives with *'* alone (*Goldilocks', Achilles'*); those of two syllables take *'s* as a rule but take *'* alone if *'s* would result in three *s, sh, z* or *zh* sounds in a row in unstressed syllables (*disease's, index's, Congress's* but *thesis', Xerxes', Bridges'*).

Roman, Italics, or Quotation Marks?

Roman, italics, and quotation marks have distinctive uses. For instance, democracy means everything we associate with that word, "democracy" means what is (rightly or wrongly) called by the word, and *democracy* means the spoken word itself.

Use quotation marks sparingly for words used in a qualified, non-standard, or ironical sense. Overuse suggests that the author does not wish to be pinned down.

Use italics for unnaturalized foreign words (those not found in the dictionary) (*CMS* 7.51). Most Latin expressions have been assimilated and are therefore not italicized. Use italics for emphasis, but with restraint; the best way to convey emphasis is by the rhythm of a sentence (*CMS* 7.49). Use italics for letters representing mathematical quantities (for example, $3x + y$) (*CMS* 14.9).

Spacing

One space, not two, should follow all punctuation that ends a sentence. This includes periods, colons, question marks, exclamation points, and closing quotation marks (*CMS* 6.11).

No spaces should follow or precede an em dash.

That or *Which*?

In choosing between the relative pronouns *that* and *which*, use *that* when the phrase in question further defines or restricts the point being made. In such cases, your ear will usually confirm the usage of *that*, because there will be no hesitation at the phrase when it is read aloud. Use *which* when the phrase, which is frequently set off by commas, simply adds information to the point being made.

> We employ an *estimation procedure that* is based on four assumptions.
>
> Equity and efficiency, *which are two primary values in modern society*, are sometimes at odds.

Use *which* whenever a preposition introduces the phrase (*CMS* 5.202).

Titles and Terms

Capitalize individual titles attached to a name (*President Reagan, Pope John Paul II*); otherwise, use lower case (*U.S. president Reagan, ex-president Reagan, the pope, the pope John Paul II*) (*CMS* 8.21).

Verb Tense

In surveys of literature, *Ripley showed* or *has shown* or *Ripley's study shows* are all correct uses of tense. Avoid jumping back and forth between the author as subject (acting in the past) and the work as subject (acting in the present). In contexts where chronology is not the focus, *Ripley shows* is correct. Authors should use past tense to describe their own procedures and results (*the respondents indicated*) but present tense to present findings (*the data indicate*). Consider the following example:

> Hart *was* clearly not *associated* with the black wing of the party, and we therefore *expect to see* Hart's vote share *diminish* rapidly as the proportion of black votes in a state rises.

Here, *vote share* and *proportion of black votes* refer to items in a model.

Citations

Brief notes on sources appear in the text as citations, providing immediate source information without interrupting the flow of argument. A citation usually requires only the last name of the author(s), year of publication (*n.d.* if it is forthcoming), and (sometimes) page or chapter numbers. The page or chapter numbers must appear unless the reference is to the entire work as a whole. All works cited must appear in the reference list at the end of the article, including those in notes to tables and figures.

The simple author-date citation is an abbreviated way of referring to the work itself. Think of it as a short title. No comma separates the two elements:

> "The transmogrifying of mayoral power" (Bailey 1987)
> For a lucid assessment, see Ripley 1988.

In the second example, a type that should be restricted to the notes, the "short title" is grammatically part of the sentence and hence not set off by parentheses. If the sentence were about the author, rather than, as here, about the work (we are not directed to see Ripley himself), the date alone would be set off by parentheses to indicate the work:

>Trish (1988) sharply disagrees.

Use embedded citations rather than notes for simple citations, including cases of "see," "see also," "compare," or similar brief phrases.

Chronology

Indicate a sequence of authors whose works form a progression of ideas through time in the text, rather than using a parenthetical citation. Parenthetical author-date citations remain a short means of reference, rather than a way of listing works in time, and should be given in alphabetical order, *e.g. Hare 1965, Singer 1963* rather than the reverse.

Multiple Authors and Works

With two or three authors, cite all names each time (*CMS* 16.117):

>(Kelly, Colter, and Lane 1980)

With four or more authors, *et al.* (in roman type) should follow the first author's name, even in the first reference (*CMS* 16.118):

>(Angel et al. 1986)

When more than one study is cited, arrange the references in alphabetical order and separate them with semicolons or semicolons and commas, as necessary:

>(Confucius 1951; Gurdjieff 1950; Wanisaburo 1926)
>(Confucius 1951; see also Gurdjieff 1950, Wanisaburo 1926, and Zeller 1914)

If two or more authors have the same last name, a first initial should be used to distinguish between them:

>(B. Ripley 1988; R. Ripley 1964)

Use a semicolon to separate two works by the same author (16.119, 2nd example):

> (Barbarosa 1973; 1978)

If works by the same author are also published in the same year, add lowercase letters to the dates of publication and repeat these in the reference section (*CMS* 16.116):

> (Frankly 1957a; 1957b)

Pages, chapters, and so forth follow the date, preceded by a comma; *p.* and *pp.* are omitted (*CMS* 16.109):

> Beaute (1975, 121–25)
> (Rex et al. 1985, chaps. 6, 7)

Older Works

For reprints, both original and reprint dates should be given (*CMS* 17.127, 2nd text citation example):

> (Marx and Engels [1933] 1964, 25)

Classics may be cited in either of two ways. The first is to use the author-date system, providing original date, publication date of the particular edition being used, and page numbers. The second can be used when standard subdivisions of the work have been established and are used in the same way for all editions. This method commonly includes the author's name, title of the work, and a series of numbers representing decreasing subdivisions of the work:

> (Thucydides, *Peloponnesian War* 2.40.2-3)

In this case, the numbers refer to book, section, and sentence. In other cases they may refer to volume, chapter, and paragraph. Citations to chapters and verses of the Bible or to numbers of *The Federalist Papers* are of the same type. Because the subdivisions are the same for all editions, no editions need be specified and the reference entry may be omitted. However, if the work exists in different translations, specify the particular edition being used and insert the year in brackets following the number series.

>(Thucydides, *Peloponnesian War* 2.40.2-3 [1963])

Government Documents

Government documents may be cited in the normal author-date form. However, many have corporate authors whose names are too long to write out each time in the text. In this case, include a short form or acronym in parentheses (or in brackets in parentheses) immediately after the first reference and use the acronym thereafter. For example, a first reference might be *U.S. International Trade Commission (1978, 12; hereafter USITC)* and the second, *USITC (1978, 16)*.

Legal Citations. An in-text citation to a statute or court case should include the name of the case (in italics except for *v.*) or statute and the year:

>(*Baker* v. *Carr* 1962)
>(Budget and Impoundment Act 1987)

Data Archived and Available at the Inter-university Consortium for Political and Social Research (ICPSR)

Citations should be modeled on the official citation provided by the ICPSR using the date of ICPSR distribution as the publication date.

For example, at the ICPSR web site the following information is given for a data set:

>STUDYNO = 6805;
>
>CITATION=Eldersveld, Samuel J., John E. Jackson, M. Kent Jennings, Kenneth Lieberthal, Melanie Manion, Michael Oksenberg, Zhefu Chen, Hefeng He, Mingming Shen, Qingkui Xie, Ming Yang, and Fengchun Yang. FOUR-COUNTY STUDY OF CHINESE LOCAL GOVERNMENT AND POLITICAL ECONOMY, 1990 [Computer file]. ICPSR version. Ann Arbor, MI: University of Michigan/Beijing, China: Beijing University [producers], 1994.

Ann Arbor, MI: Inter-university Consortium for Political and Social Research [distributor], 1996.

For an in-text citation to this study, use (Eldersveld et al. 1996) or Eldersveld et al. (1996), depending on whether the author name is part of the sense of the sentence.

Electronic Sources

In-text citations of Internet sites should be formatted to be as similar to normal articles or books references as possible. Citations should include the names of the author(s) and the year of publication, if available.

(Bruckman 1994)

(King, Tomz, and Wittenberg 1998)

Appendixes

If the manuscript draws on data not documented in standard sources or in the text of the article, an appendix describing these data may be necessary.

Authors are required to provide information about the extent of missing data and how missing data have been handled in the procedures used.

In general, an author must inform readers of any information necessary to duplicate or replicate the analysis in an article, using either the same or another data set. This information might include exact question wordings, experimental protocols, and lists of coding or recoding procedures, as well as decisions about handling of outliers, coding errors, index and scale creation or other aggregation of variables, or specific options chosen in computer programs used. The goal is to present sufficient information that another scholar can understand the precise steps the author followed in going from raw data, whether they are archived, to the tables and figures in the published article. This information can be presented in the text of the article, in notes, or in appendices as appropriate (if their presence in the text interferes with the presentation of the fundamental arguments).

For manuscripts containing quantitative evidence and analysis, authors should describe their procedures in sufficient detail to permit readers to understand and evaluate what has been done and to permit other scholars to carry out similar analyses on other data sets. It is desirable for articles to be self-contained. Authors should not refer readers to other publications for descriptions of basic research procedures such as sampling methods, question wordings, or experimental protocols.

Authors should provide complete information about sources, coding, and measurement of all variables, including complete question wording for survey data. If such descriptions are brief, they may be presented in the text or in notes, but where variables are numerous, present this information in a measurement appendix.

A useful discussion of what to include appears in Thomas Palfrey and Robert Porter's "Guidelines for Submission of Manuscripts on Experimental Economics," *Econometrica* 59 (1991): 1197–98.

Notes

Notes present explanatory material and should be used sparingly. All notes should be double-spaced consecutively at the end of the manuscript. The corresponding note numbers in the text should be typed in superscript, preferably at the end of a sentence and at least at the end of a clause. The note number should follow end punctuation (except a dash) and be placed outside a closing parenthesis (*CMS* 16.30).

Journal articles require an unnumbered "author's note" that includes the author's name, title, affiliation, a short mailing address, and an e-mail address, followed by any acknowledgments. If the paper has multiple authors, this information should be given for each one. For examples, authors should refer to a recent issue of the journal to which they are submitting. Acknowledgment of significant research assistance provided by others is encouraged. In a final manuscript, this note is placed above the first numbered note (*CMS* 16.69–16.70).

The names and version numbers of all computer programs used

for calculations and data analyses presented in the paper, as well as the specific names of procedures used should be reported in notes. If different programs or procedures are used for data presented in various tables or figures, provide the relevant information in a note at the bottom of each table and figure. If the same program and procedure is used for all analyses, that can be reported in one general endnote.

Information on citations of newspaper articles, interviews, and personal communications should be included in the notes, not the references.

Interviews and Personal Communications

These are usually best indicated in the text or in a note. Give the name of the person, the means of communication (*telephone conversation, personal correspondence, interview,* etc.), the date, and (if appropriate) the place (17.208). Electronic correspondence, including email messages and discussions via bulletin boards and electronic discussion groups, is cited as personal communication in the text.

Newspaper Articles

Include the author's name (unless anonymous), title of article, title of paper, day, month, year, and section if relevant. Do not give page numbers without also giving the edition (e.g., *eastern edition*) (*CMS* 17.188).

> Daniel F. Cuff, "Forging a New Shape for Steel," *New York Times,* 26 May, 1985.

If print and electronic forms of the article are identical, use the print version. If electronic and print versions are not the same, and the research drew on the electronic form, the note should be as similar to the print note as possible, with the addition of the URL and the date of last access, instead of the date of publication. The date of last access is used because online materials may not be permanently available:

> Vernon Loeb, "Fallout from a CIA Affidavit," *Washington Post,* www.washingtonpost.com/wp-

dynnation/A1998-2000Apr23.html (accessed April 24, 2000).

References

Citations direct attention to the more detailed references, which provide complete source information. Include no reference that is not actually cited. Be careful to refer to the most recent edition of each work used.

The examples that follow show proper forms for common kinds of references. List all references alphabetically by author (*CMS* 16.93). Give the full first name instead of an initial, unless the author is widely known by initials. Double-space all lines and indent all lines after the first in each entry. When citing several works by the same author, place them in chronological order, with the earliest publication first, but replacing the names of the successive author(s) with a 3-em dash. Repeat the name of the same author only if paired with a new author(s) (*CMS* 16.103).

If print forms and electronic forms of the material are the same, a reference for the print form is preferred, because electronic versions may not be available in all libraries or to all researchers. If electronic and print versions are not the same, and the research was based on the electronic form, the format should be as similar to that of an article or book as possible, with the addition of the full retrieval path (URL, FTP, etc.) and the date of last access. Examples are included below.

Books

One Author.

>Kessel, John H. 1968. *The Goldwater Coalition: Republican Strategies in 1964*. Indianapolis: Bobbs-Merrill.

The author's name and date—the bits of information in the citation—appear first, followed by the book title, place of publication, and publisher (*CMS* 17.26). If the city is well known, there is no need to identify the state (or D.C.) (*CMS* 17.100). Use postal acronyms for states (*MA, OH*). Chapter and page numbers should be in the citations, not the references.

Two Authors. (*CMS* 17.27)

> Sorauf, Frank J., and Paul Allen Beck. 1988. *Party Politics in America*. 6th ed. Glenview, IL: Scott, Foresman.

The surname comes first for the initial author only, and a comma, followed by *and*, separates the names.

Edited Collection. (*CMS* 17.41)

> Ball, Terence, James Farr, and Russell L. Hanson, eds. 1988. *Political Innovation and Conceptual Change*. New York: Cambridge University Press.

Chapter in Multiauthor Collection. (*CMS* 17.69)

> Hermann, Margaret G. 1984. "Personality and Foreign Policy Decision Making: A Study of Fifty-Three Heads of Government." In *Foreign Policy Decision Making*, eds. Donald A. Sylvan and Steve Chan. New York: Praeger, 133–152.

The chapter title takes headline capitalization and quotation marks. Page numbers for the chapter cited are not necessary. If the author and the editor are the same person, repeat the name.

> Crotty, William J. 1968. "The Party Organization and Its Activists." In *Approaches to the Study of Party Organization*, ed. William J. Crotty. Boston: Allyn & Bacon, 203–221.

Do not use a form analogous to this one for a chapter in a single-author book. Rather, indicate the whole book and specify the chapter in the citation.

Multivolume Work. (*CMS* 17.83–89)

> Foucault, Michel. 1980. *The History of Sexuality*. 2 vols. Trans. Robert Hurley. New York: Vintage Books.

> Foucault, Michel. 1980. *The Use of Pleasure.* Vol. 2 of *The History of Sexuality.* Trans. Robert Hurley. New York: Vintage Books.

If a cited work consists of more than one volume, give the number of volumes after the title. If the cited work is just one volume in a set, give its volume number after the title, followed by the more general title.

Publisher's Names. *The* and *Inc.* may be omitted from publisher names, as may *Press* (except for *University Press*), *Publisher,* and *Company* (*CMS* 17.104).

Journal Articles

Reference format for print journal articles includes month, season, or issue number (only one, in that order of preference). The issue identification should be enclosed in parentheses and follow directly after volume number.

> Aldrich, John H. 1980. "A Dynamic Model of Presidential Nomination Campaigns." *American Political Science Review* 74 (September): 651–69.

The article takes headline capitalization regardless of how it was handled in the actual journal.

Put the issue number in parentheses and allow one space between the colon and the pages.

Electronic Journals. Give as much of the following information as is known: author's name, document date (year), title of the article, title of the journal, any additional information provided (month and day), full retrieval path, date of last access in parentheses.

> Browning, Tonya. 1997. "Embedded Visuals: Student Design in Web Spaces." *Kairos: A Journal for Teachers of Writing in Webbed Environment* 3 (1). http://english.ttu.edu/-kairos/2.1/features/browning/index.html (Accessed October 21, 1997).

Forthcoming Work. (*CMS* 17.167)

>Jacoby, William G. N.d. "Ideology and Popular Culture." *American Political Science Review*. Forthcoming.

Unpublished Works

If an unpublished work has a sewn or glued binding, the title takes italics, like a book; otherwise, place the title in quotes.

Dissertation or Thesis. (*CMS* 17.214)

>Munger, Frank J. 1955. "Two-Party Politics in the State of Indiana." Ph.D. diss. [or Master's thesis.] Harvard University.

Paper Presented at a Meeting. (*CMS* 17.215)

>Mefford, Dwain, and Brian Ripley. 1987. "The Cognitive Foundation of Regime Theory." Presented at the Annual Meeting of the American Political Science Association, Chicago.

Manuscript in Author's Possession.

>Banks, Jeffrey S., and George Bordes. 1987. "Voting Games, Indifference, and Consistent Sequential Choice Rules." University of Rochester. Typescript.

Identify the material form (*typescript, mimeo, photocopy,* etc.) and the institution with which the author is affiliated.

Older Works

For references either to older literature that is reprinted or to new editions or translations of older (or "classic") works, include the original year of publication in brackets ([ ]) (unless unknown) along with the date of publication of the edition being used. (*CMS* 17.259)

>Burke, Edmund. [1790] 1987. *Reflections on the*

> *Revolution in France.* Ed. John G. A. Pocock. Indianapolis: Hackett.
>
> Madison, James, Alexander Hamilton, and John Jay. [1788] 1966. *The Federalist Papers.* Ed. Roy P. Fairfield. Garden City, NY: Anchor Books.
>
> Marx, Karl, and Friedrich Engels. [1933] 1964. *The Communist Manifesto.* New York: Monthly Review Press.

For reprint editions, both the original date (in brackets) and the reprint date should be given; publication information for the reprint should follow.

> Campbell, Angus, Philip E. Converse, Warren E. Miller, and Donald E. Stokes. [1960] 1980. *The American Voter.* Chicago: University of Chicago Press, Midway Reprint.

No reference is necessary unless a particular editor is specified, provided that the work has short, numbered sections to replace page numbers in the citation.

Government Documents

This section is a brief introduction to the treatment of government documents. For more detail and numerous examples, see *CMS* 17.290–356 and the latest edition of Kate L. Turabian's *Manual for Writers of Term Papers, Theses, and Dissertations*, chapter 12.

Congressional Reports and Documents. The reference begins with U. S. Congress, House or Senate, followed by any committee, year, title, Congress, session, and report or document number or committee print number. Include bills and resolutions and publications by commissions in this category.

> U.S. Congress. Senate. Committee on Foreign Relations. 1956. *The Mutual Security Act.* 84th Cong., 2d sess., S. Rept. 2273.
>
> U.S. Congress. Senate. 1934. *Report of the Federal Trade*

> *Commission on Utility Corporations.* 70th Cong., 1st sess., S. Doc. 92, pt. 71A.

Hearings. Provide the same information as for reports and documents but with the exact date in place of the report or document number.

> U.S. Congress. Senate. Committee on Foreign Relations. 1985. *Famine in Africa.* 99th Cong., 1st sess., 17 January.

Statutes. Provide the name of the statute, source (*U.S. Code* or *Statutes at Large*), volume, section, and (if relevant) page.

> Administrative Procedure Act. 1946. *Statutes at Large.* Vol. 60, sec. 10, p. 243.

Congressional Debates. The reference begins with *Congressional Record,* followed by the year, Congress, session, volume, and part.

> *Congressional Record.* 1966. 89th Cong., 2d sess., vol. 112, pt. 16.

Presidential Proclamations and Executive Orders. Provide president's name, year, title or description, *Federal Register*, volume, number, and page.

> Reagan, Ronald. 1984. Caribbean Basin Economy Recovery Act, Proclamation 5142. *Federal Register*, vol. 49, no. 2, p. 341.

Executive Department Documents. Provide corporate author, year, title, city, and publisher. If author and publisher are the same, repeat the name or use an acronym.

> U.S. Department of Commerce. Bureau of the Census. 1975. *Statistical Abstract of the United States.* Washington, D.C.: Department of Commerce.

Treaties. Provide corporate author, year, treaty name, date, treaty series (e.g., TIAS), volume, and part or number.

> U.S. Department of State. 1963. Nuclear Weapons Test Ban, 5 August. TIAS no. 5433. *U.S. Treaties and Other International Agreements,* vol. 14, pt. 3.

National Archives. Provide corporate author, title or description, file (if relevant), record group, and *National Archives.*

> U.S. Congress. Senate. Committee on the Judiciary. "Lobbying." File 71A-F15. Record group 46. National Archives.

Technical Reports. Provide author, year, title, city, publisher, and NTIS or ERIC number (if available).

> Gottfredson, L. S. 1980. *How Valid Are Occupational Reinforcer Pattern Scores?* Baltimore: Johns Hopkins University. ERIC, ED 182 465.

Legal References. List full bibliographic information for court cases in the references. (This differs from *CMS.*) Give the case, year, volume, source, page on which the case begins, and (in parentheses) district of any lower federal court. If possible, use *U.S. Reports* for Supreme Court decisions, rather than *Lawyer's Edition* or *Supreme Court Reporter.*

> *Baker* v. *Carr.* 1962. 369 U.S. 186.

> *Lessard* v. *Schmidt.* 1972. 349 F. Supp. 1078 (E.D. Wisc.).

Early in the Supreme Court's history, cases were identified by the recording clerk's name, rather than a source title:

> *Marbury* v. *Madison.* 1803. 1 Cranch 137.

Data Archived And Available at the Inter-university Consortium for Political and Social Research (ICPSR)

References should be modeled on the official citations provided by the ICPSR, making three changes to adapt them to APSA style: add the ICPSR study number to the full reference (omit leading zeros); use the date of ICPSR distribution as the publication date; and change the case of the study title.

For example, at the ICPSR web site the following information is given for a data set:

> STUDYNO = 6805;
>
> CITATION=Eldersveld, Samuel J., John E. Jackson, M. Kent Jennings, Kenneth Lieberthal, Melanie Manion, Michael Oksenberg, Zhefu Chen, Hefeng He, Mingming Shen, Qingkui Xie, Ming Yang, and Fengchun Yang. FOUR-COUNTY STUDY OF CHINESE LOCAL GOVERNMENT AND POLITICAL ECONOMY, 1990 [Computer file]. ICPSR version. Ann Arbor, MI: University of Michigan/Beijing, China: Beijing University [producers], 1994. Ann Arbor, MI: Inter-university Consortium for Political and Social Research [distributor], 1996.;

For the complete reference in the list of references at the end of a paper, use:

> Eldersveld, Samuel J., John E. Jackson, M. Kent Jennings, Kenneth Lieberthal, Melanie Manion, Michael Oksenberg, Zhefu Chen, Hefeng He, Mingming Shen, Qingkui Xie, Ming Yang, and Fengchun Yang. 1996. Four-County Study of Chinese Local Government and Political Economy, 1990 [computer file] (Study #6805). ICPSR version. Ann Arbor, MI: University of Michigan/Beijing, China: Beijing University [producers], 1994. Ann Arbor, MI: Inter-university Consortium for Political and Social Research [distributor], 1996.

Electronic Sources

Citation of references from Internet sites is formatted to be as similar to normal article or book references as possible, with the addition of their Internet addresses and the date of your last access. The latter is used because these materials may not be permanently available. To avoid citation of materials that are no longer available in this form, or incorrect Internet addresses, please check, as late as possible in the production of your article, that all Internet references can be found at the addresses given in your citations, and update the date of last access accordingly.

File Transfer Protocol (FTP) Sites. To cite text or data files available for downloading via ftp, give as much of the following information as is known: author's name, document date (year), full title of the work in quotation marks, any additional date information provided (month and day), address of the ftp site including full path needed to access the document, and the date of your last access.

> Bruckman, Amy. 1994. "Approaches to Managing Deviant Behavior in Virtual Communities." April. ftp://ftp.media.mit.edu/pub/asb/papers/deviance-chi94.txt (December 4, 1994).

Web sites. To cite text or data files that may be viewed or downloaded online through the web, give as much of the following information as is known: author's name, document date (year), title of the work in quotation marks, the title of the complete work if applicable in italics (for example, a full book title if you are citing a chapter), any additional date information provided (month and day), URL (Uniform Resource Locator or address) including full path needed to access the document, and the date of your last access in parentheses. URLs that are too long for one line should be continued on the next line without using a hyphen.

> King, Gary, Michael Tomz, and Jason Wittenberg. 1998. "Making the Most of Statistical Analyses: Improving Interpretation and Presentation." September 7. http://gking.harvard.edu/preprints.shtml (October 22, 1998).

English Translations

> Duverger, Maurice. 1954. *Political Parties*. Trans. Barbara North and Robert North. New York: Wiley.

Sources in Other Languages

Translate titles of books and articles in brackets after the foreign title; if only the English translation is given, identify the original language in brackets after the title. Do not translate the names of periodicals. For foreign language titles, capitalize only the first word and any proper nouns occurring in it (except for German, in which all common nouns are also capitalized):

> Miyamoto, Yoshio. 1942. *Hoso to kokka* [Broadcasting and the national defense state]. Tokyo: Nihon Hoso Shuppan Kyokai.

Miyamoto, Yoshio. 1942. *Broadcasting and the National Defense State* [in Japanese]. Tokyo: Nihon Hoso Shuppan Kyokai.

(For more information on foreign language sources, see *CMS* 17.65.)

Magazine Articles

References to popular magazines require the author, year, article title, magazine title, month, day (for a weekly or bimonthly), and page numbers (*CMS* 17.182–17.186).

Prufer, Olaf. 1964. "The Hopewell Cult." *Scientific American*, December, 13–15.

Tables and Figures

Tables

Tables can be a major source of confusion or can show the basis of the most important conclusions with clarity. In constructing tables, authors should be explicit about what they intend to convey to the reader. Use tables in the body of the paper to display findings, e.g., relationships or trends. Supplementary information usually belongs in an appendix. Such tables might include lists of cases included in an analysis, coding

Table 3
Accuracy of Alternative Forecasting Models, 1956–2000 (Out-of Sample Predictions)

	Actual Vote	Model 1 Prediction	Model 2 Prediction	Model 3 Prediction
1956	57.8	53.3	58.0	55.6
1960	49.9	**52.3**	**52.0**	**51.8**
1964	61.3	62.3	61.5	62.3
1968	49.6	49.4	49.0	49.5
1972	61.8	57.2	58.7	59.0
1976	48.9	47.1	**54.5**	**52.6**
1980	44.7	**52.9**	48.6	48.5
1984	59.2	57.9	58.3	59.1
1988	53.9	51.6	**49.9**	50.6
1992	46.5	43.3	44.6	43.8
1996	54.6	57.4	56.7	56.5
2000	50.2	55.4	50.3	51.1

Note: Actual and predicted votes are the percent of the two-party vote going to the incumbent party candidate. Bold entries represent cases in which the model predicted the wrong popular vote winner.

rules, question wordings, comparisons of samples and population characteristics, etc. The text must include a reference to each table, and each table presented in the main text should be discussed. Authors should study the tables in a recent issue of the journal to which they are submitting a manuscript to get a sense of the specific practices that the journal follows.

Each table should have an Arabic numeral and a title that is presented flush left, with the word Table and the title with headline-style capitalization:

Table 1. Table Style in the Journal

The table title should bear no note. Any general note should be placed at the foot of the table, with the heading *Note:* or *Source:* (a source note must be given for all previously published tables or for tables that contain data not collected specifically for this project or whose origin is not fully described in this paper). Other notes should be keyed by superscripted, italicized, lowercase letters both in the table and where the note appears.

Do not use a table to duplicate what is already in the text or can easily be explained in the text. Do not let the information in one table overlap that of another. Often two tables sharing the same row or column headings can be combined into one. Plan tables to avoid extreme width, which makes them difficult to typeset and to read.

Tables should be understandable to a reader who has not yet consulted the text or who wishes to understand the major findings by reviewing the tables but not reading the text. Therefore, tables (and their legends and notes) should contain all of the information necessary to interpret them. All columns and rows should be clearly labeled and only the most common abbreviations should be used unless a legend is provided. The exact meaning of numbers should be explained.

Column headings take headline capitalization (i.e., Headline Capitalization) and should be centered above the column, with the numbers below precisely aligned. (For numbers of grossly different magnitudes that are not being compared, e.g., Ns and percentages, align commas with decimal points.) An indication of the units used in a column may be added in parentheses just beneath the head. Place single horizontal rules across the page above and below the column heads and at the foot of the table. Do not use vertical rules and do not use horizontal rules between rows. Always provide a stub head over the left-most column. Stub heads should be flush left and take headline capitalization. Items in the stub column take only sentence capitalization. If such items have subheads, indent them approximately three spaces or ¼".

Always provide the number of cases on which percentages are calculated and indicate whether they are column, row, or total percentages. This is most efficiently done with the placement of the percentage sign, which should follow the first percentage in each column if percentages are calculated vertically, the first percentage in each row if they are calculated horizontally, or each figure in a table of total percentages (i.e., in a "three-dimensional" table where each cell is based on a different N). Supplying the figure "100%" at the bottom of each column or end of each row as appropriate is another useful visual clue for the reader. Generally speaking, it is easier for readers to interpret percentages or other figures that are presented vertically, but if the number of rows and columns in a table is such that space can be saved by presenting percentages or other figures horizontally, that should be done.

Do not carry a percentage based on samples that are small relative to their sampling frame beyond one decimal place unless absolutely necessary, as this suggests a degree of precision that such data typically cannot support. Try to round to make the rows or columns add to 100%.

Give Ns for the base number for each percentage. For columns of vertical percentages, the N for each column should be given in the bottom row of the table; for rows of horizontal percentages, the N for each row should be given in the last column of the table; for tables of total percentages (but only for such percentages), the N should be given in each cell in parentheses underneath or following the percentage figure. In the table headings or stubs, spell out the phrase *Number of cases* if space permits, although *N* is acceptable within the text of the manuscript. For statistical presentations, all figures reported should have the same number of significant digits.

Probability levels for coefficients or tests of statistical significance should be keyed by *, **, and *** in order of increasing significance (e.g., .05, .01, .001). An alternative to flagging significance is to report probability levels for all coefficients in a separate column. Report probability levels in this format even though you may have provided standard errors.

Once a manuscript is accepted or is in the final stages of revision, all tables must be collated and inserted in sequence at the end of the manuscript. Indicate the preferred placement of each table in the text (i.e., Table 5 about here). This notation should follow the paragraph containing the first text references to the table.

For more details on tables with numerous examples, see *CMS*, chapter 12.

Figures

Titles and sources for figures should follow the same format as for tables:

Figure 1. Figure Style in the Journal

Each figure should be self-explanatory, with all parts clearly labeled using headline-style capitalization. Letters representing variables take italics.

Figures must be collated and placed after any tables at the end of the manuscript. Indicate appropriate placement [i.e. (Figure 1 about here)] following the paragraph in which the figure is referred to for the first time. Each figure, too, should be self-explanatory, with all parts clearly labeled using headline style capitalization (not block capitals). Letters representing number qualities take italics. A separate sheet should be used for each figure, and copies—not originals—should be used in the manuscript. Originals are required only after a paper has been accepted for publication.

Appendix to Style Manual

Data Sources and Archived Data for Articles Accepted for Publication in the American Political Science Review

The *American Political Science Review* does not require preparation or archiving of replication data sets for data used in its published articles, although we encourage authors to do so, especially if their data are not already available. Replication data sets include all information (such as computer program options, recoding procedures, and other steps taken in your analysis) and data necessary to replicate, or build on, your published article. Authors may archive these data sets with the Publication-Related Archive of ICPSR.

If your data are available at the ICPSR, this should be mentioned either in the author's note or in a separate note and a complete reference listing should be provided. For other archives, provide appropriate information. We will not report your data as being archived unless this can be verified at the web site or in information provided by the archive. If you are reporting archiving of your data, please provide confirmatory information, such as study number or other identification.

If readers are advised that additional information is available from the author, dated and printed copies of that information should be submitted with the final manuscript. If this documentation is not submitted prior to the paper's being sent to the printer, any notes referring to such additional information will be deleted. Authors are responsible for responding to readers who ask for copies; the copy provided to *APSR* is intended only for documentation and backup. If the information that is sent to people who inquire is subsequently changed, *APSR* does not require a new version; however, authors are asked to redate any revised materials.

American Political Science Review : Submission Guidelines
Download the most current guidelines from the APSA website at: www.apsanet.org/apsr/

The APSR strives to publish scholarly research of exceptional merit, focusing on important issues and demonstrating the highest standards of excellence in conceptualization, exposition, methodology, and craftsmanship. Because the APSR reaches a diverse audience of scholars and practitioners, authors must demonstrate how their analysis illuminates a significant research problem or answers an important research question, of general interest in political science. For the same reason, authors must strive for a presentation that will be understandable to as many scholars as possible, consistent with the nature of their material.

The APSR publishes original work. Therefore, authors should not submit articles containing tables, figures, or substantial amounts of text that already have been published or are forthcoming in other places, or which are included in other manuscripts submitted for review to book publishers or periodicals (including online journals) or otherwise committed. In many such cases, subsequent publication of this material would violate the copyright of the other publisher. The APSR also does not consider papers that are currently under review at other journals or duplicate or overlap with parts of larger manuscripts that have been submitted to other publishers (including publishers of both books and periodicals). Submission of manuscripts substantially similar to those submitted or published elsewhere, or to part of a book or other larger work, is also strongly discouraged. If you have any questions about whether these policies apply in your particular case, you should discuss any such publications related to a submission in a cover letter to the Editor. You should also notify the Editor of any related submissions to other publishers, whether for book or periodical publication, that occur while a manuscript is under review at the APSR and which would fall within the scope of this policy. The Editor may request copies of related publications.

If your manuscript contains quantitative evidence and analysis, you should describe your procedures in sufficient detail to permit reviewers to understand and evaluate what has been done and, in the event the article is accepted for publication, to permit other scholars to carry out similar analyses on other data sets. For example, for surveys, at the least, sampling procedures, response rates, and question wordings should be given; you should calculate response rates according to one of the standard formulas given by the American Association for Public Opinion Research, Standard Definitions: Final Dispositions of Case Codes and Outcome Rates for Surveys (Ann Arbor, MI: AAPOR, 2000). This document is available on the Internet at www.aapor.org/default.asp?page=survey_methods/standards_and_best_practices/standard_definitions. For experiments, provide full descriptions of experimental protocols, methods of subject recruitment and selection, subject payments and debriefing procedures, and so on. Articles should be self-contained, so you should not simply refer readers to other publications for descriptions of these basic research procedures.

Please indicate variables included in statistical analyses by capitalizing the first word in the variable name and italicizing the entire variable name the first time each is mentioned in the text. You should also use the same names for variables in text and tables, and wherever possible should avoid use of acronyms and computer abbreviations when discussing variables in the text. All variables appearing in tables should have been mentioned in the text and the reason for their inclusion discussed.

As part of the review process, you may be asked to submit additional documentation if procedures are not sufficiently clear; the review process works most efficiently if such information is given in the initial submission. If you advise readers that additional information is available, you should submit printed copies of that information with the manuscript. If the amount of this supplementary information is extensive, please inquire about alternate procedures.

The APSR uses a double-blind review process. You should follow the guidelines for preparing anonymous copies in the "Specific Procedures" section below.

Manuscripts that are largely or entirely critiques or commentaries on previously published articles will be reviewed using the same general procedures as for other manuscripts, with one exception. In addition to the usual number of reviewers, such manuscripts will also be sent to the scholar(s) whose work is being criticized, in the same anonymous form as they are sent to reviewers. Comments from the original author(s) to the editor will be invited as a supplement to the advice of reviewers. This notice to the original author(s) is intended: (1) to encourage review of the details of analyses or research procedures that might escape the notice of disinterested reviewers; (2) to enable prompt publication of critiques by supplying criticized authors with early notice of their existence and, therefore, more adequate time to reply; (3) as a courtesy to criticized authors. If you submit such a manuscript, you should therefore send as many additional copies of their manuscripts as will be required for this purpose.

Manuscripts being submitted for publication should be sent to Lee Sigelman, Editor, American Political Science Review, Department of Political Science, The George Washington University, 1922 F Street NW, Suite 401A, Washington, DC 20052. Correspondence concerning manuscripts under review may be sent to the same address, or e-mailed to apsr@gwu.edu.

Manuscript Formatting

Manuscripts should not be longer than 45 pages including text, all tables and figures, notes, references, and appendices. This page size guideline is based on the U.S. standard 8.5 X 11 inch paper; if you are submitting a manuscript printed on longer paper, you must adjust accordingly. Font size must be at least 11 point for all parts of the paper, including notes and references. The entire paper, including references, must be double-spaced, with the sole exception of tables for which double-spacing would require a second page otherwise not needed. All pages should be numbered in one sequence, and text should be formatted using a normal single column no wider than 6-1/2 inches, as is typical for manuscripts (rather than the double-column format of the published version of the APSR), and printed on one side of the page only. Include an abstract of no more than 150 words. The APSR style of embedded citations should be used, and there must be a separate list of references at the end of the manuscript. Do not use footnotes for simple citations. These specifications are designed to make it easier for reviewers to read and evaluate papers. Papers not adhering to these guidelines are subject to being rejected without review.

For submission and review purposes, you may place footnotes at the bottom of the pages instead of using endnotes, and you may locate tables and figures (on separate pages and only one to a page) approximately where they fall in the text. However, manuscripts accepted for publication must be submitted with endnotes, and with tables and figures on separate pages at the back of the manuscript with standard indications of text placement, e.g., [Table 3 about here]. In deciding how to format your initial submission, please consider the necessity of making these changes if your paper is accepted. If your paper is accepted for publication, you will also be required to submit camera-ready copy of graphs or other types of figures. Instructions will be provided.

For specific formatting style of citations and references, please refer to articles in the most recent issue of the APSR. For unusual style or formatting issues, you should consult the latest edition of The Chicago Manual of Style. For review purposes, citations and references need not be in specific APSR format, although some generally accepted format should be used, and all citation and reference information should be provided.

Specific Procedures

Please follow these specific procedures for submission: 1. You are invited to submit a list of scholars who would be appropriate reviewers of your manuscript. The Editor will refer to this list in selecting reviewers, though there obviously can be no guarantee that those you suggest will actually be chosen. Do not include on this list anyone who has already commented on your paper or an earlier version of it; or any of your current or recent collaborators, institutional colleagues, mentors, students, or close friends.

2. Submit five copies of manuscripts and a diskette containing a PDF file of the anonymous version of the manuscript. If you cannot save the manuscript as a PDF, send a diskette with the word-processed version. Please ensure that the paper and diskette versions you submit are identical; the diskette version should be of the anonymous copy (see below). Please review all pages of all paper copies to make sure all copies contain all tables, figures, appendices, and bibliography mentioned in the manuscript and that all pages are legible. Label the diskette clearly with the (first) author's name and the title of the manuscript (in abridged form if need be), and identify the word processing program and operating system.

3. To comply with the APSR's procedure of double-blind peer reviews, only one of the five copies submitted should be fully identified as to authorship and four should be in anonymous format.

4. For anonymous copies, if it is important to the development of the paper that your previous publications be cited, please do this in a way that does not make the authorship of the submitted paper obvious. This is usually most easily accomplished by referring to yourself in the third person and including normal references to the work cited in the list of references. Under no circumstances should your prior publications be included in the bibliography in their normal alphabetical location but with your name deleted. Assuming that text references to your previous work are in the third person, you should include full citations as usual in the bibliography. Please discuss use of other procedures to render manuscripts anonymous with the Editor prior to submission. You should not thank colleagues in notes or elsewhere in the body of the paper or mention institution names, web page addresses, or other potentially identifying information. All acknowledgements must appear on the title page of the identified copy only. Manuscripts that are judged not anonymous will not be reviewed.

5. The first page of the four anonymous copies should contain only the title and an abstract of no more than 150 words. The first page of the identified copy should contain (a) the name, academic rank, institutional affiliation, and contact information (mailing address, telephone, fax, e-mail address) for all authors; (b) in the case of multiple authors, an indication of the author who will receive correspondence; (c) any relevant citations to your previous work that have been omitted from the anonymous copies; and (d) acknowledgments, including the names of anyone who has provided

comments on the manuscript. If the identified copy contains any unique references or is worded differently in any way, please mark this copy with "Contains author citations" at the top of the first page. No copies of submitted manuscripts can be returned.

Perspectives on Politics : Submission Guidelines
Download the most current guidelines from the APSA website at: www.apsanet.org/perspectives/

Perspectives on Politics is a general journal of political science that seeks to provide political insight on important problems, as it emerges from rigorous, broad-based research and integrative thought. The editors anticipate authors and readers primarily comprising political scientists, but also including journalists, policy analysts, public officials and their staff, and other social scientists. The articles aim to clarify for such an audience the political significance of accumulated research regarding a particular area of the world, an important policy problem, a deep normative conflict, or a significant institution or process; they may also demonstrate the insights that accrue from viewing politics from a distinctive viewpoint, method, or type of evidence.

Articles in *Perspectives on Politics* will enable members of different subfields of political science to speak to one another--and with knowledgeable people outside the discipline--on issues of common interest. To do that, they must be conceived differently from most articles in political science journals. Those typically address the author's peers in a specialized area and thus can presume that readers use the same tools and terminology and know the general context and significance of the author's query. By contrast, in Perspectives each article must be meaningful for people with much general knowledge of politics but with no specific knowledge of the issue at hand.

Contributors may take a variety of approaches, illustrated by but not limited to the following possibilities:

- Explaining what central political issues are at stake in a given topic of research (such as classical Greek philosophy, the development of an independent judiciary, the nature of politics in a particular country or region, campaign finance reform, or state involvement in international trade). An article in this vein should show why those issues matter to a wide audience and how the reader should understand the issues in light of particular evidence, history, frameworks, or values. It will probably also explain what problems remain to be studied or cannot be resolved. Such a piece may offer a distinct, even contentious (but well-defended) stance rather than a neutral or carefully balanced judiciousness, so long as it fairly articulates opposing viewpoints. Alternatively, it could offer a broad summary of an emerging research subfield or bring together disparate sets of literature that are mutually illuminating. Several articles that represent varied viewpoints, types of evidence, epistemological frameworks, or conclusions and recommendations could be combined into a symposium or other type of structured exchange; we invite proposals for these.

- Showing what political science can offer to help people understand a crucial political event or tendency (such as the rise of religiously inspired political terrorism, illegal immigration from poor to wealthy nations, or the demand for democratic elections). What does the academic study of politics and power teach us that journalists, political actors, or insightful observers cannot? Where appropriate, authors are encouraged to offer recommendations for political action, moral judgment, or policy choices as a way of demonstrating the distinctive contributions of the discipline of political science to the problem at hand.

- Showing how a multiplicity of individual research projects in a given area, once suitably organized and connected, adds up to a major shift in our understanding of some important aspect of politics. Artfully crafted and thematically oriented review essays of major books and articles are the most obvious and appropriate way of accomplishing this task. Authors could also review Web sites, political speeches, general exam reading lists, collections of syllabi, novels or plays, museum exhibitions, pieces of campaign literature, legal decisions, legislative debates, or any other phenomenon that enables political scientists to reconfigure settled understandings and focus on new questions or arguments.

- Reflecting on conceptual developments within political science in order to show how the study of politics and power has changed, whether for better or worse. Authors may trace the development (or distortion) of a crucial concept or theory, perhaps across several generations of scholars; examples include theories of racial formation, pluralism, modernization, political economy, political culture, or justice. Senior authors might reflect on their earlier work, noting what they would have written differently had they known then what they know now. Younger scholars can discuss the relevance of "classic" works to their current scholarship.

- Reflecting on conceptual links and divergences across space rather than across time. How is an idea such as rights, gender, democracy, the market, or security used differently in different countries, political parties, epistemological frameworks, or social science disciplines? Why do these different usages matter for our understanding of politics?

- Taking on perennial unanswerable (or at least unanswered) questions about power and politics, and showing how political scientists can contribute to at least partial answers. How can political scientists make sense of sin and evil, or virtue and inspiration? Why did communism fall in most nations of the world and at a particular moment? What are the political implications of the huge movements of persons and capital around the world? Why do states repress or make war on people within their own borders? Why is capitalism closely associated with democracy? (This is, of course, a small sampling of potential topics.)

- Reflecting on how the knowledge generated by political scientists affects and is affected by academic and political infrastructures. Studies of libraries, foundations, university and college departments, or teaching priorities may shed light on how and why the study of some political phenomena has flourished or withered, or why some methods of analysis grow or disappear; they should also show how this affects our understanding of politics and power. A related question considers how knowledge produced by political scientists is used, or misused, by people outside the discipline" and what types of knowledge policy makers, journalists, social scientists in related disciplines, and political activists wish academics would produce.

In short, what unites articles in Perspectives on Politics is that all political scientists and many public actors can learn from them. Nonspecialists will become aware of the most important research in a subfield and the most intriguing questions opened up by that topic. For specialists, articles should lead to new questions about their ongoing research and teaching, new ideas about how to proceed, and new connections with other arenas of the discipline or other disciplines. Scholars in related disciplines will see how they can use research on politics and power in their own work, and how they can contribute to our agendas. Political and policy actors will find their positions and proposals supported, challenged, and changed by evidence emerging from broad-based research; they too are welcomed as contributors. All of us will learn more about why and how the discipline of political science matters.

Style, Format, and Types of Articles

These goals have stylistic implications. Perspectives has several types of articles, organized into distinct sections. In the "Articles" section, authors generally follow the traditional model of an academic journal by using the results of research or analysis to address a political problem or phenomenon, with a focus that is broader than the usual report on an individual research agenda. These articles can be as long as 16,000 words. In the "Perspectives" section, authors may offer short, sharp commentaries on a political phenomenon or policy problem; engage in dialogues or debates to highlight methodological or substantive disagreements; or provide insights into or evaluation of other works of interest to political scientists. These articles can be as short as five journal pages. In the "Review Essays" section, authors may review a small set of books, articles, or other "texts" in order to show how these materials illuminate a larger conceptual, political, or normative concern. These articles range in length, averaging about 10 journal pages.

Whatever the length and format, all articles must aim simultaneously to appeal to nonspecialists and to convey distinctive insights to specialists. An article will typically begin with a few paragraphs introducing the topic, its importance, and the gist of the central argument. Alternatively, the author may set up a fascinating puzzle or raise a stimulating question, and invite the reader to follow a line of argument to a resolution revealed only at the end. In either case, at crucial points of transition the author should recapitulate and foreshadow; the conclusion should make crystal clear just what readers have learned.

Avoid jargon when possible. Since Perspectives aims to maximize readership and appreciation of each article, please take great pains to use the simplest and most straightforward method of exposition possible in making an argument (authors will be able to provide links to more detailed or technical material). Specialized vocabularies and equations are appropriate if explained in the text and essential to a topic or argument. Perspectives especially welcomes illustrations, charts, and other visual material that help to explain an important point. Articles must be well written, tightly organized, and lively. Be sure that all endnotes, references, and appendices are essential rather than decorative or defensive.

Procedures for Submission and Review

Perspectives on Politics uses several channels to generate and develop articles. The editor and associate editors solicit some. Potential contributors may send either a proposal or an article draft.

You can e-mail your proposal or draft as a Microsoft Word or WordPerfect document to popsub@mail.rochester.edu, or mail three copies--double-spaced, 12-point type on one side of the page--to this address:

Perspectives on Politics

Political Science Department

University of Rochester

Rochester, NY 14627-0146

In all cases, be sure to save a copy of the document for yourself, and include all contact information for the author(s): name, title, address, e-mail, phone, and fax. Please also indicate the word count as well as the subfield(s) of political science into which your proposal or manuscript falls.

Proposals

Proposals should include the following:

- an informative and provocative proposed title;
- an engaging lead paragraph, designed to appeal to as wide an audience as realistically possible;
- a summary, abstract, or outline of no more than 1,000 words, including a statement of the topic, research base, framework for analysis or interpretation, and central insights or conclusions;
- a separate statement to the editorial staff, if appropriate, on the distinctiveness of this topic, approach, style of presentation, or anything else;
- an anticipated (rough) word or page count for the proposed draft; and
- if the proposal is for a review essay, full information on the articles, syllabi, etc., being proposed for review.

Our editorial team will discuss each proposal; for those that seem promising, the editor or an associate editor will give initial reactions and invite a draft. The editors will assess the draft; if they decide that it might be a good fit for Perspectives, they may make suggestions for revision before sending the manuscript to two or more external reviewers who have had nothing to do with its development. Based on those reviews, the article will be accepted, sent back for further revisions, or rejected. Authors retain final say about content and wording of articles; the editor makes the final decision on whether to publish.

Draft Articles

Those who submit draft articles--like those who submit proposals--should be sure to include an inviting title, an engaging lead paragraph, a clear statement of purpose and content, and a sharp conclusion. Additionally, they should provide an approximate word count at the beginning of the document, number all text pages consecutively, number charts or illustrations separately, and put each chart or illustration on a separate page. Notes and references should be double-spaced at the end of the article, not cited parenthetically within the text. References in Perspectives articles are limited to works cited. Bibliographic endnotes are abbreviated in, "Smith 2002, 49-56"--and are interspersed with informational endnotes.

The process for review and acceptance of submitted draft articles is similar to that of proposals. For those that seem promising, the editors may provide suggestions for revision. When the article seems close to completion, it will be sent to two or more reviewers who have not been involved in the development of the piece. Further revisions may follow that review, at which point the editor will make a final decision.

Conflict-of-Interest Rules

(Proposed and confirmed by the 6 editors, May 2002)

1. Editors will not publish an article or review essay in Perspectives, either as author or as coauthor, during the time that they serve on the journal's editorial board. However, they may be called upon to do other kinds of writing for Perspectives, such as introductions for symposia.

2. Editors will not assume chief responsibility for editing/developing articles or review essays submitted by their departmental colleagues or students. This goes for both (or all) departments if editors hold joint appointments. They may offer comments on articles by their colleagues/students; they may also solicit articles from colleagues/students or encourage colleagues/students to send manuscripts to another editor. Editors will not be primary decision-makers when it comes to accepting or rejecting manuscripts submitted by their colleagues or students.

3. Editors will not solicit review essays about books or articles that were written by their departmental colleagues or students, and they will not be primary decision-makers when it comes to accepting or rejecting such essays. They may offer comments on such essays in draft form; they also may suggest to another editor review essay ideas that include books or articles by colleagues or students.

4. Rules #2 and #3 also hold for former students who obtained their Ph.D. five or fewer years from the date of a proposal or submission.

5. Rules #2 and #3 also hold for anyone who has worked as a coauthor with an editor within five years of a proposal or submission.

6. Although all recommendations by external reviewers and associate editors will carry a good deal of weight, the editor-in-chief has final say as to which manuscripts are accepted for publication.

Final Words

Perspectives on Politics aspires to be engaging, illuminating, provocative, and broad-based; it seeks to build bridges across the discipline of political science and to reach out to fellow social scientists, people directly engaged in political action, and people who are simply interested in politics. Its articles should be useful for students, specialists, nonspecialists, practitioners, and kibitzers. Perspectives seeks to be experimental in content and format while retaining the highest standards of scholarly excellence. The editors warmly invite suggestions for articles, symposia, review essays, commentary, and dialogues, as well as other ideas, from political scientists or anyone else concerned

PS: Political Science & Politics: Submission Guidelines

Download the most current guidelines from the APSA website at: www.apsanet.org/ps/

PS is the journal of record for the American Political Science Association. The journal provides coverage of the broad range of observations and information about the discipline. Its coverage has evolved since its introduction in 1968 to include critical analyses of contemporary political phenomena by authors working within their own subfields aimed at the informed, general reader.

Editorial Guidelines

* Submissions should be manuscripts that have not been published previously and are not under consideration for publication elsewhere.
* Manuscripts should present issues and analyses of relevance and interest to political scientists with clarity and conciseness. Good writing matters.
* Qualitative and quantitative manuscripts are welcome. However, manuscripts that are exclusively descriptive or that rely heavily on methodological and statistical presentations are not suitable for publication in this journal.
* The subjects and methods of articles should be of interest to political scientists reading outside their own field of interest or specialty.

Manuscript Guidelines

* Submitted manuscripts are subject to a blind-review process of approximately 2-3 months in length. Authors must submit their manuscripts through the journal's online manuscript processing system, found here: http://mc.manuscriptcentral.com/pspsp. New authors will need to create an account within the system before submitting their manuscript. The author's or authors' name(s) should appear only on a separate cover sheet, and the first page of the text should include the title of the manuscript. Language within the text that might identify the author(s) should be avoided.
* When submitting a manuscript through the online system, the author will need to have the following information available: three keywords that describe the manuscript; a cover letter available to upload or cut-and-paste; an abstract of no more than 200 words; the number of words in the manuscript; the number of figures, tables, and graphs in the manuscript. After uploading your manuscript, make sure you view it in both pdf and html before logging out of the system. Finally, authors may submit works in progress through the system to work on over time before submitting a final version for peer review.
* Materials reproduced from already published work must be accompanied by permission of the original publisher or copyright holder.
* Manuscripts should include in-text citations that will correspond. Endnotes and references should conform with the APSA Style Manual for Political Science and the Chicago Manual of Style.
* Manuscripts should be double-spaced and formatted for 8 1/2" x 11" paper and should not exceed 15 pages in length.
* Gender-specific pronouns used to refer to members of the profession or to society at large should be avoided.
* Manuscripts submitted for possible inclusion in the "front" of PS--Symposia;

Features; The Teacher; and The Profession--may be submitted at any time. Except with Symposia submissions and a few extraordinary cases, authors cannot submit manuscripts for inclusion in a particular issue. Accepted and revised manuscripts are customarily printed in the next available issue, themes and page count permitting.

* Authors addressing especially timely and topical subjects are encouraged to contact the editor before submitting their manuscripts. Special provisions can be made to "rush" an article or set of articles through the review process.

Manuscript Processing and Production

* Upon submission, the editor makes an initial judgment about the suitability of the manuscript for publication in PS. Suitable manuscripts are sent to a minimum of two reviewers. After reviewers make their recommendations, the editor reaches a final judgment. Every effort is made to limit the review process to three (3) months.

* If the editors, based upon the recommendations of the reviewers, feel that the article would benefit from revision the author(s) will receive a letter from the editors asking the author to revise the article as outlined by the reviewers and to resubmit it for further review by the editors and, perhaps, other reviewers. The author(s) has one year from the date of this letter to resubmit a revised version of the article. Revised and resubmitted articles over a year old will not be considered for publication in PS.

* Once accepted, authors are asked to submit a revised final copy of the manuscript. A statement transferring copyright from the author to the American Political Science Association is necessary before publication. The editor will provide the necessary copyright transfer form.

* The final copy is copy-edited and returned to the author for final approval. All changes and revisions are incorporated into the manuscript electronically and submitted to the printer.

* One set of page proofs is sent to the author. Corrected page proofs should be returned to the assistant editor within two (2) days of receipt of the proofs. Every effort should be made to limit corrections to typographical errors. Fees charged for other changes will be the responsibility of the author.

Symposia

* Individuals wishing to submit a set of articles for a symposium or to organize a group of scholars on a topic should first consult with the editor about the theme and prospective authors.

* The editor may also invite authors to submit articles addressing a single theme or question. Invited articles are also subject to the review process.

Submission

Submit manuscripts through the online system at:
    http://mc.manuscriptcentral.com/pspsp

Submit questions to: ps@apsanet.org

Resources on Teaching, Learning, and Professional Development on...

Teaching/Learning

Teaching Resources

Political Science Syllabi

Links to Online Teaching Resources

Essays from "The Teacher"

Distance Learning in Political Science

Service Learning in Political Science

Civic Education

Civic Education in Political Science

APSA-CIVED: Civic Education Discussion List

Professional Development

Graduate Student Connection

Preparing Future Faculty

eJobs: Online Database of Jobs in Political Science

Professional Development Resources

Careers in Political Science

Precollege Teaching

Precollege Teaching Resources

Guidelines for Training Elementary and Secondary Teachers

Teaching Political Science

www.apsanet.org